Small Business SEO & Local SEO Ranking Strategies

Quickly Rank Your Businesses Website For The Keywords That Matter To Your Bottom Line

Shane David

Free Download Area

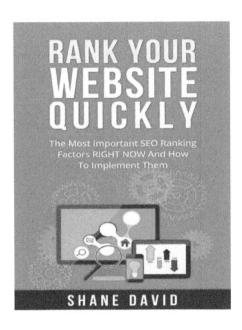

Wait A Minute! Rank Your Website Even Quicker With This Free Gift

As a token of my gratitude for purchasing my ebook, I wanted to give you a small, but very valuable gift. I've been doing SEO full time now since 1998 and I know better than anyone else how quickly things change when it comes to SEO.

But there is one time proven strategy that always works and that ranks your website for the keywords that matter quickly.

Grab your free gift below and implement these strategies today. **You will learn;**

* The ONE strategy that will almost always guarantee you high rankings

* The new rules of SEO – Google knows more about your site than ever before

* An instant rank boosting SEO strategy that you can implement in minutes

http://thefulltimer.com/seo/

Table Of Contents

Introduction

I began my SEO career back in 1998, before Google was a thing we all loved to hate and before SEO was even a widely used term.

I have been the head of SEO for two digital media agencies and have been responsible for thousands of 1st page rankings for local & small businesses all over the world.

I wrote this book for anyone looking to improve their businesses website rankings, and at the end of the book, you will have all the knowledge you need, to be able to do your own SEO confidently.

I will be teaching you a 4 step method to ranking for local keywords, that is used by just about all of the GOOD quality SEO agencies.

(There are so many bad SEO services and companies out there, but I'll get to that in a moment).

That 4 step process is;

Keyword Research, Relevancy Auditing, On-Page Optimization and Business Branding.

This 4 step process is a proven, natural and safe way to rank for even the most toughest or stubborn keywords and while the process might sound complicated, it is however very simple and quick to implement and I'll walk you through the entire process, step by step.

The ideal student for this ebook is a small or medium sized business owner who knows the value of SEO to bringing in qualified leads and business and who wants to take control of their own SEO marketing instead of having to pay thousands to expensive agencies, hoping they actually know what they are doing.

Maybe you are a local dentist, or a small manufacturing company, or the local beauty salon, maybe you run a timber company with locations in a few different cities or states and you want an affordable way for customers to find you.

I can think of 1000+ businesses who would benefit from the SEO knowledge in this guide. This course will even allow you to stop spending hundreds if not thousands of dollars a month on Google Adwords.

Small Business SEO is also perfect for those who want to start doing local SEO for businesses in their local area and who need an up to date course on what's working now.

All of these strategies are completely safe, whitehat SEO strategies. Nothing here goes against what Google wants, in fact, our entire goal IS to give Google what it wants.

There are a few strategies in this guide I've found no where else. Some of the strategies so called "experts" would disagree with me on. My expertise comes from nearly 20 years of experience and literally thousands of top 10 rankings for small business and local SEO keywords.

The Importance Of Controlling
Your Own SEO Destiny

Once you learn the skills of doing your own SEO, you will never be left in the dark again about why or how to rank your businesses website for the keywords that matter.

If you've had any experience with SEO agencies, you know they make the process sound as difficult as possible. This is simply so you don't try and attempt to learn or do it yourself.

When you can generate leads for your own business, with your own knowledge, that is when you will never have to worry about finding customers or clients again.

It baffles me why so many small business owners leave something so important to their businesses success up to other people.

This is a KEY skill to have.

Yes, it takes a bit of know how and a bit of trial and error, but there is a very simple, step by step process to ranking your businesses website for the keywords that matter to your business.

The role of this guide is to help you find the keywords that have the best chance of improving your businesses bottom line. It's not about working for vanity metrics.

What's the point of doing this work to get people to your website who are not interested or are only slightly interested in what your business has to offer?

No point.

We want to find the most relevant keywords so we can find the customers and clients your business needs, that have cash in hand, ready to purchase.

They are looking for what you are offering, in your location, ready to purchase. That's what this guide is all about.

Finding those people and making sure you are front and center in their minds and their search results.

When you can do this yourself, without having to rely on outside parties, this is when you take control of your businesses destiny, instead of leaving it in the hands of people, who quite honestly, often don't care about your businesses success.

At the very least, they don't care as much as you do about your business and it often shows in the results.

Why Hiring An SEO Company Can Be The Worst Thing To Do For Your Small Business

I must first say, not all SEO companies or agencies are bad or evil. That's not true and I don't want that to be the impression I give.

What is true is that;

A) They are always expensive

&

B) They don't care about your businesses success as much as you do.

Those are simple facts.

What is very common is people pretending to be SEO experts. Even big SEO firms hire people straight out of university with absolutely no SEO experience and put them on the front lines.

They give them a basic checklist of things to do to your site and hope for the best. There is a term in this industry for that group of people, SEO Monkeys.

Because they do tasks you could hire monkeys to do and charge you an arm and a leg. Most of their practices are outdated and often harmful to your website.

This is not all SEO agencies, but a very big majority. Another large group of people or businesses who offer SEO services are website designers.

Just because someone has a lot of experience designing websites, that does not mean they are SEO experts.

Usually that's always the case. Website design businesses offer SEO services to jump on the bandwagon.

It's something they can collect money for and not have to do a lot for as they don't have the required skills to do the job properly.

The problem is, clients don't always know what a good or bad job is when it comes to SEO.

Small and local businesses also can't afford to pay monthly retainers for these SEO services, regardless of quality.

It's hard to find $500 to $1500 a month, every month and quite frankly, when it comes to local SEO, you don't need to do a lot of monthly maintenance to maintain your rankings.

That's another very big scheme SEO agencies use to get you hooked. Pay us monthly or your SEO rankings disappear.

If you do local & small business SEO right, you should only have to do a few touchups every 6 months or so, depending on the keywords you choose for your business.

The 4 Steps To Ranking For Local & Small Business Keywords

There are 4 major steps to ranking for local keywords. Those are;

* Assessing Your Current SEO Situation & Getting Your Website Ready

We need to find out where you are ranking now, what SEO has been done to the site already if any, how much traffic you are getting and from where, what your social media profile looks like.

We need to setup Google analytics, social media accounts, check your websites speed and health. It's important to know where you are before we get you to where you want to be.

It's also important to make sure your websites health is AOK first, otherwise you will just be wasting time.

* Find The Keywords To Rank For That Will Bring You Streams Of Customers Or Clients

In this step we will create a keyword tree. (Easy To Do). This keyword tree will list out your most important keywords to your least important keywords so you can focus on the low hanging fruit first.

We will be using a free tool to find these keywords. We will also be doing some competitor analysis.

Looking at who your main competitors are and seeing where they are ranking for what keywords and why.

Keyword research is vital to your SEO success. Keyword research and relevancy are the two big keys.

We need to find the keywords that you can rank for and that are the most relevant to your business.

* Making Your Site The Most Relevant Site For The Keywords You Are Targeting

One of the major factors to good rankings in Google is how relevant you are to the keywords you want your site to target.

Google will deliver you 98% of all search engine traffic that comes to your site, so it's important we give them what they want.

It's not about tricks or schemes that work for weeks or months.

We give Google what they want and they give us better rankings. Giving Google what they want is all about giving your visitors what they want.

Relevancy.

There is no use ranking for a keyword that gets a lot of searches if it's not even closely relevant to what you sell or offer. It's about customers and clients in the door, not vanity metrics.

In this step, we are going to turn your site into the most relevant search result, and we do that through content and on-page optimization.

Very simple strategies any one can employ. We are also going to look at your mobile readiness as well.

* Branding Yourself As The Goto Business In Your Niche / Area / Location

In just about every area or city or niche, or all of the above, there is a business that when you say their name, people instantly recognize what they do.

That's what you want to be.

Why? Because brand is HUGE with Google and SEO in general. You've probably heard of back linking. Getting other websites to link to yours to help boost your rankings.

Quality links are a good thing, but people get so focused on acquiring links, they forget about where they are coming from. Quality over quantity.

Google also frowns on heavy handed link building tactics. That's what a lot of the recent updates were about. Penguin and Panda. A LOT of businesses got caught out with this.

A LOT of SEO agencies got caught out and hurt their clients rankings with these un natural linking practices.

Our goal, in this step, is to get YOUR brand known online and we do that with a few different methods. The more well known you are, the more NATURAL links you get back.

We do this through outreach, content creation, social media and simply asking for links in a natural way.

Assessing Your Current SEO Situation Through A Quick Audit

It's important before we start doing any sort of SEO to your site that we first do a quick assessment of where you are currently.

If you are creating a new site and using the information in this guide to build your site, not all of this will apply to you.

If you are wanting to use the strategies in this guide on a website you have had now for a while, all of this applies to you.

Here are a couple of things we need to check first.

Are You Indexed?

By this I mean, is your site already listed (listed or indexed is different from rankings) in Google. We can find that out easily. Go to Google.com and type in;

Site:yoursitenamehere.com

Obviously change yoursitenamehere.com with your actual web address. Don't add the http://www. infront of it.

This will show you all the pages on your site that are currently indexed in Google. That simply means, Google knows about your site and those pages.

Good first step.

If your site has been around for any length of time, you will no doubt see a list of results. How any pages are indexed will depend on how many pages in total your site is.

Sometimes not every page of your site will be listed here, and that's usually fine. There will often be pages on your site that really don't serve much of a purpose to be indexed for.

If you know your site has many pages and you only see 1 or 2 of your pages indexed, that could mean something is wrong.

Same goes if you don't see your site at all. If your site has been around longer than a few months, this would be a bad sign.

I'll talk more about this shortly.

Are You Ranking For Any Keywords?

If you have not done any sort of SEO work to your site, it's very likely your not ranking for any meaningful keywords, but it's best to find that out now so you know exactly where are you.

If you are, it's a good thing, if you are not, no harm is done.

To do this, we can use a paid tool, which has a limited free option. No signup is needed to use this tool. Just head over to;

SemRush.com

This tool will show you where you are ranking for keywords with any amount of search queries per month.

It is limited quite substantially if you have the free option.

If your businesses website has a lot of rankings, you won't be able to see them all as they limit each query.

I recommend the tool, but it's not cheap at around $69 per month.

So go to the site above, select the country your site belongs to. If your site targets the US market, select US on the right, otherwise choose your country that your business belongs to.

Put in your website address, but leave out the http://www.

Just type your website address like this;

businesssitehere.com

Adding the http://www. Will give you the wrong results for this search.

Press search and what will come up is an overview of the keywords you are ranking for and how much search traffic you are currently getting.

If you scroll down the page and click on 'full report', where it says 'top keywords' it will give you more keywords.

You can see the keywords you are ranking for by search volume and by % of the traffic they are bringing to your site.

When you change these options, you get to see more keywords you are ranking for as well, so I'd recommend playing around with the results.

Choose between ascending and descending order to see more results.

These numbers are a rough overview, not an exact science. What we want to find out however, is as many of the keywords you are ranking for.

This tool gives you lots of data.

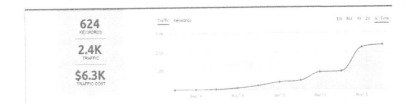

That's what a good looking SemRush chart should look like.

It tells you how many keywords you are ranking for, (they only search the top 2 pages of Google.com), how much SEO traffic you are getting (very rough figures, very) and how much that traffic would cost to buy with Google Adwords.

What you should do now is jot down all the keywords you are ranking for in an Excel file or some sort of database so you can keep track of where you are and where you are going.

These are the things I'd jot down.

Keyword – Search Position Your Site Is On – Page That Is Ranking For That Keyword – Search Volume Of That Keyword

Do that for every keyword you can find and mark down the date you are doing this so you can see the improvements over time.

If you purchase the full version, you can see the full results.

Have You Done Any SEO Work Before On Your Site?

This is important to find out. Have you or anyone associated with the business done any sort of SEO work to the site? Have you hired anyone?

If you hired someone, find out EXACTLY what they did. This is quite important, especially if you find you are penalized.

It's most likely you are not penalized, but we still need to find these things out.

Are You Penalized?

A Google penalty means you have done something with your site that Google frowns upon.

That might be keyword stuffing (using the same keywords over and over again on your pages on your site to try and game the search engine) or using bad backlinking methods.

When you have a penalty, it either affects your entire site or select pages of your site.

It basically means your site won't be moving up the search engine rankings any time soon with Google.

This guide won't work with penalized sites. That's a whole other category, not covered in the scope of this guide.

Good news is, your site is very unlikely to be penalized and it won't be penalized if you've never done any sort of SEO work using bad, old school tactics.

If you have been penalized, you need to speak with the person who did the SEO work on your site and ask them to fix it.

If you are penalized, you can ask Google for a reconsideration through your Google webmaster tools account (I'll get to that in a minute), but they won't reconsider it until you've fixed all the issues.

It's not always plain to see if your site has a Google penalty or not.

If your site is not indexed or only one or two pages are and you've had someone do SEO work on your site previously, it's very likely you have a penalty.

Here are some good resources on what penalties are and how to recover from them;

https://sites.google.com/site/recoverfrompenalty/

https://blog.kissmetrics.com/recover-from-any-google-penalty/

Now,

The other problem could be if for some reason, your site is set to 'noindex'. This is a piece of html meta tag code that asks search engines not to crawl or index your site.

The likely hood of this being set this way is low, it would have to be done manually by your website designer and there are not a lot of reasons to do this other than when the site is being built and your designer doesn't want Google and other search engines to index and crawl your site until it's finished.

There is a quick way to find this out. Go to your website and check all your important pages for this code;

<META NAME="ROBOTS" CONTENT="*NOINDEX*, NOFOLLOW">

You can do so in your Internet browser. Go to your website, right click anywhere on your site and click "view source". This will bring up all your html code. Use the 'find" tool to look for that code.

If your code says,

<META NAME="ROBOTS" CONTENT="*INDEX*, FOLLOW">

that's what you want. If it says noindex, nofollow, you or your website designer or webmaster need to change that ASAP.

Do You Show Up In Google's Local Placements?

These are the search results that look like this when you type in a local key phrase like; Eyebrow Threading Chicago;

Lakeview Threading Salon
www.lakeviewthreadingsalon.com
4 Google reviews · Google+ page

(A) 739 W Belmont Ave
Chicago, IL, United
States
+1 773-348-0250

Designer Perfume Outlet & Eyebrow ...
designerperfumeloop.wix.com
4.7 ★★★★☆ 10 Google reviews   Google+ page

(B) 28 E Madison St
Chicago, IL, United
States
+1 312-332-5750

Threading Plus
www.threadingplus.com
2 Google reviews

(C) 899 S Plymouth Ct
Chicago, IL, United
States
+1 312-566-9194

Dorthy's Eye Brow Threading
plus.google.com
2 Google reviews

(D) 5908 S Archer Ave
Chicago, IL, United
States
+1 773-884-0188

Brows Threading
browsthreading.yolasite.com
3 Google reviews · Google+ page

(E) 606 W 31st St
Chicago, IL, United
States
+1 312-808-0773

Perfect Eyebrows
plus.google.com
2 Google reviews

(F) 2828 N Clark St # 12
Chicago, IL, United
States
+1 773-281-3852

THREAD AWAY INC
www.threadaway.com
4.4 ★★★★☆ 10 Google reviews · Google+ page

(G) 500 N Wells St
Chicago, IL, United
States
+1 312-670-2513

Map results for eyebrow threading chicago

Those are the local placements. The other search results are what are called organic search results.

The SEO work we do to your site really only affects yours organic search result rankings.

But, you can also get into Google's Local Placements as well, which I'll talk about below. We just want to make sure if you are there or not now.

Now, not all industries or businesses will fit this bill. If you offer a local service, you may very well be able to get listed here.

To check this, work out what the major keyword would be for your business. Are you a dentist in Spokane? Type "dentist spokane" (without the brackets) into Google.

Are you in the local placements? Are their local placements for your search result? That's not always a given.

If you are a national company, local placements may not be for you unless you have an actual physical address in that city or location.

If you can get into those listings, you should and I'll discuss this further shortly, but this guide is mostly geared towards organic search engine rankings.

Getting Your Website Ready
For Better Rankings

Now we need to get your site ready for rankings. What goes on behind the scenes of your businesses website is just as important as what your visitors see.

Before I start this section, if you had someone design your site or do your web marketing, you may need to contact them and ask them a few things.

These are the steps you should take before moving on to doing SEO work on your businesses website.

Google My Business

Remember those local listings I talked about earlier? This is where you can set that up. Google My Business.

https://www.google.com/business/

I'm not going to go into great depth here as Google has a great FAQ and walk through for you already and I'd only be repeating what they say, poorly.

You want to setup a My Business account and you want to fill out as much of the information as they give you.

This is also where you need to ask the person who did your marketing or website setup if they've already set this up for you.

If you see your business in the local placements already, it most likely means someone has setup an account for your business.

You are going to need these details.

If you are doing it for the first time, like I said, Google has a great page for you to learn everything about their local placements.

https://www.google.com/business/befound.html

Here is another really good guide on setting up your My Business and Google+ profile page. This talks a bit about the importance of keywords and photos. You should read this;

http://www.newedgemarketing.com.au/setup-google-my-business/

They also give you a very good idea on how to get the all important reviews from your customers.

I'll be talking about this later as well.

If your business is in multiple locations around your country or state, you can also use this service for all your locations.

You really want to make sure that the contact address and phone number and business name that is on your website is also 100% correct in your My Business account.

This is a negative ranking factor if they are mismatched.

Google Webmaster Tools

This is where Google can talk to you about your websites search health. Google can send you messages through your Google Webmaster Tools account.

This is especially useful if you are unsure if you have a penalty or not. Google sends notices to your Webmaster Tools account if you have received a manual penalty.

This is also where you can go to submit a reconsideration. It's an important account to have.

https://www.**google**.com/**webmasters/tools/**

This is also where you can go to submit your websites sitemap, which is very important and I'll discuss further below.

It also gives you updates on where you are ranking for keywords as well as a rough metric of how many clicks per day you are getting from Google.

There is a lot more to it as well, but those are the features that will most interest you. You will also need to find out if you have a Google Webmaster Tools account before you create a new one.

It's a very easy tool to setup. One thing to note is, it will ask you what country is specific to your business.

If you do all your business in one country, make sure to choose that country, not the default, which I believe is the United States.

Google Analytics

This is optional, kind of. You don't need it, but you would be crazy not to signup for Google Analytics. Again, ask if you have this setup or not.

Google analytics is a free analytics tool that shows you how many visitors a day are coming to your site, where they are coming from, what pages they visit, how long they stay, what time of the day they came and a bunch more really cool stuff.

This is very very helpful to building a great SEO site in my opinion. This kind of data is invaluable.

Here is a step by step guide to setting up Google Analytics and more about the functionality.

http://www.wordtracker.com/academy/learn-seo/analytics/set-up-google-analytics

Creating A Sitemap

A sitemap is a file or document you put on your site that lists all the pages on your site. It helps search engines crawl and find all the pages on your site better and quicker.

It's a really important function to have on your site and you want to submit this in your Google Webmaster Tools account.

It's a very simple and quick process and I have a step by step guide for you below on how to do it;

http://www.wordtracker.com/academy/learn-seo/technical-guides/how-to-create-sitemap

Website Speed & Errors

A major factor for SEO rankings now is your websites speed. How fast does your site load when someone clicks on it in Google.

If your site loads slowly, your rankings will decrease.

Google only wants sites that give a great user experience for their visitors. Why would they want to rank a site that takes forever to load?

The answer is they don't and visitors to your site won't wait around for it to load. I've seen a lot of local and small business websites that are just completely clunky.

They are loaded with flash pages, huge images, slow loading graphics, you name it. Your site should be nice and clean and professional looking.

It should load quickly, be easy to navigate and the text should be easy to read. You should keep your images on the small to medium size. No fancy flash loading pages.

I had a client whose website took 30 seconds to load. On purpose. It was a bunch of flashing, arty images on the screen.

They sold hair care products to retailers.

Do you think retailers want to wait around for that?

No is the answer.

They want the information they want and they want it now and for it to be easy to find otherwise they will just go to your competitors instead.

Google has a tool to show you how fast or slow your site loads and what is causing your websites slowness.

It's called Google Page Insights.

https://developers.google.com/speed/pagespeed/insights/

Just put in your website address where it asks for it and press 'Analyze'. It will come back with something like this;

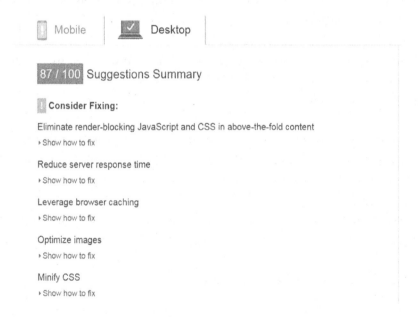

It will give you a speed score out of 100 and will tell you what you can do to improve your sites speed. You can do this for all the important pages on your site.

If you are in the green, that's great. If you are in the orange, you should think about fixing the issues that come up. Red, you definitely need to fix up your websites speed.

This is something you will need to take to your website designer and show them the results you are getting. It's not acceptable to be in the red.

Most of the time you can increase your sites speed by;

A) Compressing the images on your site to make them smaller.

B) Upgrading your websites hosting account to a better server.

This tool will also tell you how your site is going on mobile devices, which is super important and I'll talk more about that shortly.

Location And Phone Number

It's very important for local businesses to have their address and phone number and even email address on every page of their site.

It's important for visitors to your site and it's important for Google My Business listings. Make sure you put your details on every page of your site, even if it's just in the footer of your site.

Domain Name & Website Hosting

You already probably have a domain name and website hosting, but I will give you a few quick tips.

If you are looking to buy a domain name, pick a country specific domain name if you are outside the US.

If you are inside the US, .com is the only way to go. Nothing else really works like a .com.

If you are outside the US, find your local country domain extension and register with that. In Australia, it's .com.au, in the UK, it's co.uk & .uk, in New Zealand it's .co.nz and now also .nz, in Canada it's .ca and so forth.

If you are outside the US and you sell to your local market, IE in your country, always use your countries specific top level domain name extension over .com or any other extension.

If you want to get the .com of your business name, go for it. Always a good idea to protect your brand online.

Now, website hosting.

If in the Google Speed Test tool it's coming back that your server is responding slowly, that most often means your website hosting, or the server your site is on is very slow.

It's crucial that your site loads quickly as I discussed earlier. This may mean you need to upgrade your website hosting plan with your current webhost, or it may mean you need to find a better website hosting company.

Cheap hosting may look appealing, but there is a reason why it's cheap. For a small or local business, you should be looking at spending around $10 to $20 a month for your hosting.

You don't need a dedicated server or even a virtual private server. Shared hosting is fine, you just need to find a good quality hosting plan.

Talk to your current hosting company about your concerns, see if they have anything to fit your needs, otherwise you may need to move.

When I'm setting up a local businesses website, I look to spend around that $10 to $20 a month range.

HostGator.com has a website hosting package for businesses starting from around $11 a month.

If you are outside of the US, I'd recommend finding a local website hosting company.

This will help when you need support, and also there are SEO benefits to hosting your site on servers residing in your country of residence.

I personally would never host a site in the US unless I was targeting US search results. There is some merit to this and every little advantage helps in the SEO game.

Mobile Is 50% Of The Game – Are You Responsive?

Between 40% and 60% of traffic coming to a local or small businesses website is coming from a mobile device. Whether that be a mobile phone or tablet. Mostly, it's mobile phones.

Google launched a new update recently that negatively affects websites which are not responsive. A responsive website is one where the site changes automatically to fit the size of the device the visitor is using.

Old HTML sites are not responsive. Most Wordpress sites are.

You can check with Google if your website is responsive here;

https://www.google.com.au/webmasters/tools/mobile-friendly/

If you find you do not have a responsive website, it's absolutely critical that you get this fixed ASAP.

This doesn't usually involve getting a whole new site developed, you can get a mobile site developed separately, which will automatically redirect mobile visitors to this new mobile site.

This is something you can discuss with your website designer and should cost no more than a $100 to $200 dollars depending on the size of your site.

Any recently created website will more than likely be mobile responsive. If not, it is something you need to fix. Don't spend many hundreds or thousands fixing the problem, it should not cost that much.

You can even do it yourself with the help of a paid tool;

http://onbile.com/

As I said earlier, with the latest Google update, it's very important that your site is responsive otherwise you are already behind the eight-ball to begin with.

If you are doing LESS than your competitors are doing, why would you then expect to rank higher than them in the search engines?

Introduction To Keyword Research – Find The Keywords That Matter To Your Small Businesses Bottomline

When someone does a search in a search engine like Google.com, that's a keyword. These are pure gold and exactly what we need to find.

We need to find the keywords that people are searching for when they are looking for your service or product in your location(s).

It isn't about ranking for every keyword. It probably isn't even about ranking for the keywords you THINK you should be ranking for.

It's about ranking for the keywords that will bring you in the most targeted leads with the minimal of work.

You want to rank your website for the keywords that your customers and clients are looking for you for.

Nothing else matters. Keyword research is not as tricky as it sounds.

We have a couple of tools that we use to find the best keywords and a very simple method of working out what keywords are the best for your business.

I'll also be showing you a way to find out where your competitors are ranking and for what keywords so we can use their own data to your advantage.

(Perfectly legal, all SEO companies do this).

Not All Keywords Are Created Equal –
Get This Wrong And It's All Over

Targeting the wrong keywords for your businesses website can be the kiss of death for your SEO efforts.

You would be better off targeting no keywords and doing no SEO to your site than doing this step wrong.

Keyword research is about relevancy.

Finding the most relevant keywords for your business. A lot of people assume that the most searched for keywords are the ones you should be ranking for.

Not always so.

Let's say you run a beauty salon in Denver. The keyword 'Beauty Salon' gets a ton of searches per month. Is it the best keyword to rank for?

No. It's too vague and too competitive.

'Beauty Salon Denver' and or 'Beauty Salon In Denver' are the better choices. That's a very simple example, but it holds true.

Those keywords are more relevant to your business and they are a lot easier to rank for. Instead of trying to compete with every beauty salon in America, compete for the lesser competition keyword that is also more relevant.

Target the keywords for those who are in your location and looking for what you offer are searching for. It's a simple concept that a lot of businesses complicate and get wrong.

Be relevant to your target demographic and you will be rewarded for that.

Another example. Let's say you offer hairdressing services. Do you want to rank for 'hairdressing styles', which gets hundreds of thousands of searches a month, or 'Hairdresser Denver', which is the most searched for keyword when people are looking for hairdressers in Denver with over 500 searches a month?

Hopefully, you realize by now it's the second option.

How To Build A Profitable Keyword Money Tree – Google Keywords – SEMRush Competitor Keyword Analysis

In this section, we are going to use a couple of different tools. The Google Keyword Tool and SEMRush.com again. Both tools are free to use for what we need.

Before we get started, I'd suggest getting a notepad or opening up a text document on your computer so you can start to write down the keywords we find for your business.

To use the Google Keyword Tool, you will need to signup for a free Adwords account with Google.

They require this to use the tool. You don't need to spend any money on advertising or put in any credit card at all.

https://www.google.com.au/adwords/

Simply signup for a free account and follow the steps. It takes all of 5 minutes to do this. You don't need the Google Keyword Tool if you pay for the PRO paid version of SEMRush.com.

I still recommend doing this step however as the Google Keyword Tool is very good as well and of course it's free to use.

Once you signup for your Adwords account, you can start using the search tool here;

https://adwords.google.com/KeywordPlanner

Sign in using your Adwords login details. You will come to a screen like this;

Keyword Planner

Where would you like to start?

Q Find new keywords

> Search for new keywords using a phrase, website or category

> Multiply keyword lists to get new ideas

Ⅱⅼ Plan your budget and get insights for keywords

> Get search volume data and trends

> Get click and cost performance forecasts

You want to click on the 'search for new keywords using a phrase' link. Now we can start searching for keywords. Where it says 'your product or service', that's where you want to put in your keywords.

Before you do that however, you want to change the location settings, maybe. Let me explain.

If you are a local business, you will want to change the location to your COUNTRY. If you are in the United States, change it from all locations to the United States. Don't drill down any further.

Don't drill down by state or city, which you can do, but we don't want to.

If you are in another country, select that country from the drop down menu. This will give you the search results from that country, not from everywhere in the world. Very important you do this step.

If you are a global business or don't want to target specific locations, leave this on all locations.

Now, for the moment, you don't need to change any other settings. In fact, I'd leave all settings as they are in the future, especially if you are new to this. Best not to complicate a simple process.

Now you want to put in some keywords into the keyword search area. This is where you will want to create your keyword money tree and you will need to take notes.

A keyword tree is all about finding the right keywords for all the services or products you sell. Some keywords will require their own branches, while others can fit together.

Let me give you an example using the beauty salon in Denver example we used earlier. What I do for my clients is I ask them the following questions;

* What keywords do you think your customers are using to search for you?

* Name all your relevant services you offer in order of importance to your business

* What locations are you in? Tell me the state, city and suburb.

Now that's a good start. With the beauty salon in Denver, here is how I see their initial keyword tree from their perspective.

* Beauty salon denver, denver beauty salon, beauty salon in denver, hairdresser denver, denver hairdresser, makeup artist denver, denver makeup artist.

* Teeth whitening, hairdressing, eyelash extensions, eyebrow threading, waxing, makeup artistry, spray tanning, nails,

* We have no other locations

Now we have a set of base keywords to work with. You should be doing this at the same time for your business.

If you are not a local business, don't put in a city or location. If you have multiple locations, do this for every location you are in.

So currently, our keyword tree looks like this;

Beauty Salon Denver

Teeth Whitening Denver

Hairdressing Denver

Hair Extensions Denver

Eyelash Extensions Denver

Eyebrow Threading Denver

Waxing Denver

Makeup Artistry Denver

Spray Tanning Denver

Nails Denver

We now need to put these keywords into our keyword search tool. I don't recommend putting them all in at once, you will get a confusing amount of search results.

So for now, I'll put in 'beauty salon denver' & 'salon denver'. Once you do that, you will be taken to another page. You want to click on the tab that says 'keyword ideas'.

Ad group ideas	Keyword ideas

This will now take you to a list of relevant keywords that we now need to sort through. It will give you the keywords and the search volume. That's all we need to worry about now.

I'm going to write down the most relevant keywords below and explain why I chose what I chose.

Then we will need to do this for every seed keyword we came up with before for our initial keyword tree.

Salon Denver – 880 (this number represents approximate search volume per month).

Beauty Salon Denver – 30

Nail Salons Denver – 880

Hair Salons Denver – 880

Nail Salon Denver - 260

Hair Salon Denver – 320

Salons In Denver – 260

Best Hair Salons In Denver – 390

Hair Salons In Denver – 170

Best Hair Salon Denver – 140

Tanning Salons Denver – 260

Beauty Salons In Denver – 140

Best Nail Salon Denver – 260

Nail Salons In Denver – 110

Ok, so those are the most relevant keywords I could find. I try and stick above about 70 searches per month in terms of search volume. Unless the keyword is really specific and for a service that doesn't have a lot of other search terms, then stick above about 70 to 100 searches per month.

If it's a service or product that you make a very tidy profit from and 30 to 50 visitors to your site a month would be a significant profit boost for you, then go for it.

Right now, for this keyword, we don't want to include things like, hair salon, nail salon, tanning salon Denver, etc. Those we will bunch with their services on the keyword tree.

So right now my keyword tree looks like this;

Beauty salon denver, salon denver, salons in denver, beauty salons in denver.

m going to crank out the rest of the keyword tree for you now. is will take me about 20 minutes, but I've literally done tens of nousands of these, so it could take you quite a few hours to get a complete tree done.

Take your time.

Write down all the keywords and their search volumes and then create your keyword tree like I did above.

Beauty salon denver, salon denver, salons in denver, beauty salons in denver,

Teeth whitening denver, laser teeth whitening denver, denver teeth whitening,

Hair salons denver, hair salon denver, best hair salons in denver, hair salons in denver, best hair salon denver,

Hair extensions denver, denver hair extensions,

Eyelash extensions denver, denver eyelash extensions,

Eyebrow threading denver, denver eyebrow threading, eyebrow shaping denver, threading denver,

Waxing denver, denver waxing, eyebrow waxing denver, male waxing denver,

Makeup artist denver, denver makeup artist, wedding makeup denver, permanent makeup denver,

Spray tan denver, best spray tan denver, tanning salons denver, tanning denver, airbrush tanning denver, spray tanning denver

Nail salons denver, nail salon denver, nails denver, nail salons in denver, best nail salon denver, denver nail salons, nail salon downtown denver, nail salons downtown denver,

-

There you go. Sometimes you think a keyword will be the one you want to rank for, then you do some keyword research and you find out you are completely wrong.

That's why guessing what people are searching for to find you is a mugs game. That's what most small businesses do, so you are already ahead of the curve.

Even in an industry and location that I have no personal involvement in, I was still able to find great keywords. Since you live this day in day out, your keyword tree will be even better than mine no doubt.

A Simple Way To See What It Will Take To Beat Your Competitors

Now to just make sure we've not forgotten any keywords, lets go spy on your competitors. Use the keywords above to find the sites ranking for the keywords you want to rank for.

Simply type the keywords into Google and look for the websites that are ranking in the top 10 organically for those keywords. Organically means not the local placements we talked about earlier.

Now go back to SEMRush.com and use the country your business is in.

First thing you want to do is type in your competitors main URL into SEMRush.com, IE;

WebsiteHere.com

This will show you the keywords they are ranking for all throughout their site. You can see what keywords they are ranking for and where. This is super useful as you can now find keywords you might not have thought about.

Now, if you want to drill deeper, you can go specific to a page on their site. Let's say they are a salon in Denver and they have a page on their site about teeth whitening. You can copy and paste that url into SEMRush.com and see their rankings just for that page.

To search for specific pages of a competitor, you need to add the http:// in front of their domain name, otherwise SEMRush will only show you a high level keyword report for their entire domain and we want to look specifically at this one page and where it's ranking and for what keywords.

You can do this for all your competitors and like I said, it's all perfectly legal and above board.

-

Now you have done your keyword research and you know where your competitors are ranking as well. Make sure you write all your keywords down somewhere safe and make sure you get your keyword tree done like I did mine.

Now it's time to make your site the most relevant for the keywords we have found.

Introduction To Relevancy – One Of The Major Local / Small Business SEO Factors

It's all well and good to have great keywords selected, but if your businesses website isn't relevant to those search terms, you are not going to rank anywhere.

That's why relevancy is so important. It's not sexy, it's not backlinking or keyword research, it's writing content and making your site something Google wants to rank well and of course the other minor search engines as well.

Google is always our main target. They will bring in 98% of your traffic, in terms of search traffic that is, so it's very important we play by their rules.

With the keywords we chose above, you should have a page on your site for each branch. The top branch are the keywords you want to rank your homepage for, and the branches below that are the pages on your site.

You want to make sure each page is relevant to the branch chosen and I'll get into this more in a moment.

We want to make your site the most relevant for all the keywords we've chosen.

The Factors That Make Up Your Sites Relevancy

Here are the factors that make up your sites relevancy;

Your location (if applicable to your business)

Your content

Your url structure

Your chosen keywords

If you are creating a new site, some of this will be easier for you to do than if you were applying these strategies to an older site.

For example, URL structure is something you can't really change for older sites. You can add new pages, but you can't really modify old pages to change their URL structure unless you are wanting to strip your website back and start again.

Which may be an option, it's up to you. Let me explain.

When it comes to your location, we've talked about this at length already. You only want to target keywords that are in your location. No use targeting cities or states where those people searching couldn't visit you or purchase from you even if they wanted to.

Location may not be a problem for your business if you are national or global.

Content is the next big thing. I'll say it right out front now. The more quality content your page has and your site has, the better rankings you will get.

Let's say, using the example of the Denver beauty salon, that we want to rank for 'Spray Tan Denver'. Now let's say that your competitors have on average 750 words of content on the pages they are ranking for that keyword.

If you come in with 750, 1000, 1500 or even 2000 words of content, you are going to blow them out of the water already.

Content length alone with good keyword research is often enough to rank for the toughest keywords. You need to do more than your competitors. Simple as that. Can't skimp. This was one of the biggest sells I had to do with clients.

They didn't understand that more, HIGH quality content meant MUCH better rankings. Take the time and or money to do this right and you will be rewarded.

It will mean you will have to do less leg work in the future when it comes to backlinking and trying to get your name out there.

Content is key with Google. If you skimp on this step, or are planning on skimping on this step, stop reading this book, because I can't help you.

Good quality, lengthy, relevant content, with great keyword research, optimal on-page SEO and some quality backlinks thrown in, that's a recipe for top 10 rankings right there.

I'll be covering more of this in a minute.

Next is URL structure.

URL structure is simply what your pages are called.

For example; YourDomainHere.com/eyebrows1234

That's an example of bad URL structure for the keyword 'Eyebrow Threading Denver'. Good URL structure would be;

YourDomainHere.com/eyebrow-threading-denver/

If you already have a site up and running, it's not advisable to change your URL structure unless you are happy to lose whatever rankings you have now.

You will need to delete those pages to start over. You should never have 2 pages for the same or similar keyword. That will end up in your two pages competing in Google for the same keyword and it's also frowned upon by Google.

You would either need to start again, or leave your URLs as is. You can of course create new, better URLS for keywords you have not targeted yet.

It's not 100% imperative to do this. You can absolutely rank without this sort of URL structure. A lot of businesses don't use this URL structure, but I find it helpful.

Having your keywords in the URL is helpful right now. Some people say that it's over doing it, but I've never seen that in the thousands of first page rankings I've achieved for myself and the businesses I work with.

I would always recommend making every part of your site the most relevant it can be. I don't believe in keyword stuffing or gaming the search engines, but having a relevant page URL is none of the above.

It's helping your visitors know exactly what your page is about.

It's a different thing to have an URL structure like that above and then the content doesn't match what you promised. You can't create an optimized page about Eyebrow Threading In Denver, then write about hairdressing.

That's a big no no and it goes against being relevant.

Relevancy is KEY. You can get away with a lot more optimization when you are RELEVANT and the best search term for that keyword.

We want our sites to the be the BEST search result for those keywords we are targeting.

Of course, the last thing is our keywords. We've already talked a great deal about this, so I won't go over that again. We should only use the relevant keywords for the relevant pages on our site.

The On-Page SEO Strategies That Boost Your Relevancy Score

Now we are going to talk about making your pages on your site the most relevant they can be and what On-Page SEO strategies work really well.

Good thing is, most of your competitors won't do half this or even any of this.

Now let's tall about relevancy score. Let's assume Google has a relevancy score of MAX 100. Meaning you can do on-page SEO strategies that boost your relevancy score to a max of 100.

Here is how I score my strategies for relevancy.

Keyword Selection – 25%

High Quality, Lengthy Content – 25%

Optimized Title Of Page – 15%

Optimized Url Structure – 10%

Sprinkling Relevant Keywords Naturally In Your Pages Content – 10%

Optimized Heading Tags In Content & Meta Description – 5%

At Least One Quality Keyword File Name Optimized Image Per Page - 5%

In-bound Linking To Other Pages On Your Site – 5%

Other factors come into play as well, that I've discussed earlier, like your location, website speed, coding errors, website server location and mobile responsiveness, but this is what we can focus on now concerning each of the pages on your site.

Let's get into making your pages as relevant and optimized as possible.

Keyword Selection – 25%

We've already covered keyword selection in-depth and it's 25% of the on-page relevancy score in my opinion. These numbers are my own, not official numbers from any search engine or Google for that matter.

This comes from my own experience.

Have your keyword tree ready for the next steps.

High Quality, Lengthy Content – 25%

I'm going to talk more about this in the next section, but high quality content is king. This and good keyword research / selection is 50% of the battle right there. Even if you do everything wrong, you could still rank with just these two factors done properly.

The pages on your site should be laid out nicely, the content should be easy to read. You should use shorter paragraphs where possible and a rule of thumb I use is, if your competitor has 750 words of content on their page, write 1500 words.

If they have 1000 words, write 2000 words. Double what they do is always a good rule of thumb, but I talk more about this and why you shouldn't write just for the sake of word count below.

Optimized Title Of Page – 15%

Your title of your page is massively important. It's what is shown at the top of your sites browser, it's the main text people will see when they search for you in Google and your search results comes up.

It's also a massive ranking factor in Google.

Again, it's all about being relevant.

One thing to keep in mind with your title, is the length. No more than 50 to 60 characters long, otherwise Google won't display it properly and will use what it thinks is your relevant title.

So let's say we are working on two pages right now, your home page and using the beauty salon in Denver example again, we are also working on the page about makeup artistry.

This is how I write my title tags;

(Keep in mind, I'm not going into how to change your websites text. This guide isn't about designing your website, it's about doing your SEO.)

There are plenty of free guides or paid ebooks on Kindle about designing websites.

Most Relevant Keyword | Business Name

Here is the example for the home page;

Beauty Salon Denver | Business Name Here

Let me explain. Salon Denver is the most searched for relevant term for my home page. My home page will be about my entire beauty salon business, not a specific service or product.

I added beauty in front of it as that adds another longer keyword naturally to the title. The longer the keyword is, called long tail keywords, the easier those keywords are to rank.

This gives us the ability to rank for another (2 total) keyword naturally, which will give us more visitors per month if we rank for it.

You want to use the keyword that is the best and most relevant for your title as your title gives you a big SEO boost for that keyword.

So use your best, most relevant keyword or keywords for your titles. That title now targets the keyword, salon Denver & beauty salon Denver.

Now for the makeup artistry title page, I would use this;

Makeup Artist Denver | Business Name Here

Simple enough. It's the best keyword and I couldn't really naturally add another word in front or behind that. I like to use the exact keyword in the title, within reason and as long as it sounds natural.

You don't want to over do this. You could use something like this;

Makeup Artist In Denver | Business Name

That sounds a bit more natural, but I still use the exact keyword in the title tag. As long as it's relevant, I see no problem with that and I've done this for many years now and I've seen many Google updates and penalties and live through them all unscathed.

If you want to play it safe, add in an extra word to the keyword to make it sound more natural. Beauty Salon In Denver, Makeup Artist In Denver.

Don't add too many keywords in the title or make it sound really un-natural, Google will slap a penalty on you if you do that.

Don't stuff your title tags with keywords like this;

Makeup Artist Denver | Makeup Artists Denver | Denver Makeup Artist |

You are asking for trouble if you do that. Pick your best keyword and fit it in naturally. If you can get two in naturally as a long tail keyword, even better.

I also include the business name of the business as well. This is for branding purposes which becomes more important later on down the track.

I like to use the | key to separate the keyword from the business name. Makes it look clean and natural. I'd suggest always using the pipe | key for this.

If the keyword you chose for your title doesn't sound natural in it's keyword form, make it sound natural by adding in another word if you need to.

Optimized URL Structure - 10%

In my opinion it's better to have this;

domainhere.com/eyebrow-threading-denver/

Than,

domainhere.com/eyebrowsdonewell/

It's more relevant. Again, don't over do the keywords and keep it short. I'd recommend using the title tag keyword as your URL.

If you have an old site, I wouldn't recommend changing the URL's you currently have. You can add new pages like this, but leave the old ones.

If you are building a new site, I'd definitely recommend using a keyword based URL.

Remember again, each set of keywords from your branch should have its own page. If you have 10 services, you should create a separate page for each service, with it's own URL and unique content.

Sprinkling Relevant Keywords Naturally In Your Pages Content – 10%

This is where the rest of the keywords come into play that you chose earlier. You want to naturally sprinkle them around in your content and this is made easier if your content is longer as you can fit in more keywords naturally.

I don't recommend using your keywords in their current form. So for example, instead of saying something like this in your content,

We consider ourselves as one of the best beauty salons Denver,

You would say this;

We consider ourselves as one of the best beauty salons in Denver.

More natural and the keyword of 'beauty salons Denver' is still there, Google can see that, but it's natural.

Your content should always read naturally. A visitor should not be able to see where you've tried to place your keywords in your actual content.

If they can do that, you are doing it very wrong.

You want to naturally add these keywords into your pages. Keyword stuffing is a thing of the past.

Trying to get your keywords on your page as many times as possible is another negative ranking factor in Google and something you want to avoid.

You can use your keywords once each in different variations to make it more natural. It's not about how many times you use these keywords, it's about making them fit into the pages content organically.

If in doubt, use each keyword in a natural tone twice per content page. It really doesn't matter about frequency, more about relevancy and fitting into your content naturally.

With this method, not only will you start ranking for your main keyword, you will also start ranking for these extra long tail keywords as well, which can often bring in just as much traffic as your one main keyword.

Optimized Heading Tags In Content & Meta Description – 5%

There are HTML tags that create headings in your pages content. H1, H2, H3, H4, etc. They match up with the sizes of your words.

Google puts an emphasis on the words in your headings. They figure these are the more important keywords on your page and deserve more attention.

I'm not going into how to create these tags in HTML, again, this is about SEO, not website design, but I will show you how to use them properly.

Also, most Wordpress sites / themes automatically add your H1 heading to your site as your title tag you added in earlier, which is what you want.

You don't want two H1 headings on one page.

You should have one H1 heading on your page. This should be the title of your page that we talked about earlier.

H1 headings are very important and should be used for your main keyword or keywords.

H2 headings are also important. I use these to break up the page so it doesn't look like one big wall of text. You should be using your secondary keywords in your H2 headings where it's possible and natural to do so.

Again, don't flat out use your keyword as is if it doesn't sound natural. I break up the content on my page with H2 headings.

They allow me to clearly identify different sections in my content for easier reading and of course, the SEO benefits I just mentioned.

H3 headings are less important. I don't use these often unless I need a subheading for my H2 heading. It's just another way to format your page. I try and stick with just H2 headings where possible.

Let me give you an example, using the beauty salon in Denver example.

These are the keywords I want to use on this page;

Teeth whitening denver, laser teeth whitening denver, denver teeth whitening.

My H1 heading would include the keyword Teeth Whitening Denver.

Then I'd break up the page with 2 H2 headings.

Laser Teeth Whitening Denver

&

Denver Teeth Whitening

Examples;

We Offer Laser Teeth Whitening In Denver

&

Our Denver Teeth Whitening Services & Our Prices

At Least One Quality Keyword File Name Optimized Image Per Page - 5%

Images in your pages are important. I'd recommend at least 1 image per page and probably 2 if the content is longer than 1500 words. Too much content looks like a brick wall of text and that's not something you want for good user engagement.

Images increase social sharing and the amount of time a visitor stays on the page. Very important stats. It's also a good chance to get another, if not small, ranking factor into the equation.

What I mean by that is, you can make the file name of your image or images your important keywords. This is a small ranking factor.

You could call your image, Teeth-Whitening-Denver.jpg and that gives you another chance to get your keyword on the page, while also adding a much needed image to your content.

Make sure to only use high quality images, images that you have taken yourself or have copyright usage for. Never just take an image from the web and use it on your site, you will very likely get sued.

I like to put an image at the top of the page and half way down the page. Also make sure the image is relevant to your pages content. Don't put a picture of a puppy on a page about your teeth whitening services.

In-bound Linking To Other Pages On Your Site – 5%

Another on-page ranking factor which is also very easy to do is linking between your pages on your site. You can and should link pages together naturally.

When I work on a clients website, I usually put 2 inbound links on a pages content to other pages on their website. This not only helps with SEO it also helps visitors navigate your site easier.

What I mean by interlinking is this.

Somewhere in your content, you naturally place a link to another page on your site. For example, on a page about our eyebrow threading services, I'd write something like this;

"If you are after eyelash extensions to go with your amazing new eyebrows, we also offer a no appointment required eyelash extension service."

Now my eyebrow threading page is linking to my eyelash extension services page naturally. What you don't want to do is overuse this tactic or use overly keyword rich inbound link text.

For example, I wouldn't make the link the words;

Eyelash Extensions Denver

That can look like keyword stuffing to Google, even in small doses. You want your links to look natural, because they are natural.

Content Creation - You Just Need To Do More Than Your Competitors

Unique, high quality content is key to this method working. Whatever is on your businesses website, it must be of a high quality, relevant and lengthy.

If you have trouble writing content, hire a college student to do it or hire a professional. Either way, it has to be done.

Some will say content length doesn't matter all that much for small business or local SEO, but I can tell you now, it plays a huge part in your rankings.

I've run hundreds of experiments with short and long content and I'm not saying short content doesn't rank, it certainly does, especially for less competitive keywords, but long content still blows short content out of the water.

It also plays a huge part in your rankings for long tail keywords. Those extra keywords we found that were not your title tag. The longer your content, the more times you can mention those long tail keywords in your content.

When I do work for clients and I look at their analytics and rankings, a good chunk of the time their long tail keywords combine to bring in more traffic then their main keywords they chose.

Long content and long tail keywords are very important. The longer the keyword, usually the easier it is to rank for.

Most of your competitors are down-right lazy and have not done the sort of keyword research that you've now done. You are many steps ahead of them.

They go after the most obvious keywords, not the best keywords.

When it comes to content length and quality, you need to do more than your competitors. Search for your keywords, see who is ranking and look at what they are doing content wise.

How many words is it? How long is it? Do they do all the on-page work we've talked about earlier?

You NEED to do more than your competitors who are ranking high for the keywords you want to target.

You don't want to do JUST enough, you want to blow them out of the water. Don't do a bit less than them and expect better results. Don't do as much as them and expect better results, because it won't happen.

You need to do MORE. More words, higher quality. Quick tip about word count, if you want to know how many words are on a websites page, try this tool;

http://www.seoreviewtools.com/bulk-web-page-word-count-checker/

It will check the word count of the page for you.

One more thing I will add.

Studies have shown time and time again, that content which is longer than 1500 words, ranks exceptionally better than content which is under that amount. There is no competition really.

2500 words is the optimal number, but I'd aim for 1000 words minimum. That will keep you in very good standing.

You don't want to put in text or content for the sake of it. You don't want to be repetitive or put in words just to get to a certain word count, that's a big no no.

If you feel you've added everything you can of value to a page with the content you have, then that will have to be enough, but it's extremely important to try and get that word count up.

A Simple Way To See What It Will Take To Beat Your Competitors

Remember, when it comes to keyword research and competition, we are looking at the organic rankings, not the local placements we talked about earlier.

There is a very simple way to see if you can beat your competitors without having to get technical or use any tools to check for numbers and stats.

It takes no more than 5 minutes to do this for each set of keywords you've chosen. Simply use the checklist I've shown you above and see if your competitors are using the same tactics.

For example, if a good chunk of your competitors in the top 10 of Google for your main keywords are not using those keywords in their title tags, there is a very VERY good chance you can rank for that keyword.

Same goes for content length. If their content is short, you are VERY likely to rank for these keywords even with a brand new site and no backlinking or off-page SEO done to your site.

If everyone in the top 10 is using all or the majority of the SEO tactics I've discussed so far, you will find it more difficult to rank for these keywords.

Not impossible however. Far from it. It just means you are in a competitive market.

Most of the time however, and I'd say this is 98% of the time, your competitors are not using proper title and H1 headings for their main keywords, their content is short, their website loads slowly or isn't responsive, they don't use long tail keywords in their content and their URL structure is poor.

Introduction To Branding Yourself As The Go To Business In Your Niche & Area

Quite frankly, using the tactics I've already discussed above is often enough to rank for even some of the most toughest keywords. That's how powerful it is, but when you add in off-page SEO as well, things start to get really interesting.

Off-page SEO isn't something you can do in a day or a night, or even a week. It's a life time thing that you do every once in a while to keep your rankings going strong. It's something that will actually just become a part of your businesses promotional activities.

The more you promote your business through traditional channels, as well as online, the more you brand your business and the higher your rankings will go.

There is no need to GAME or TRICK search engines. It's a fools errand.

When people think about off-page SEO or link building, they think about getting as many links as possible and usually links with their keywords stuffed into them as many times as possible.

That use to work 5 years ago, but will get you slapped hard now by Google and other search engines. It's not even something you should contemplate.

What I explain to my clients is that we are not looking to get as many backlinks as possible, we are trying to BRAND their business as THE place to go for X service or X product.

There is always one business in a niche or location or industry that people know by name. "Oh yah, I know so & so business, they do X".

Those businesses NATURALLY attract links back to their websites. It's a snowball effect and that's what you want to do for your businesses website.

It's not about hustling backlinks from people, it's about branding yourself as THE place for X, whatever X may be in your instance and that's what I'm going to show you how to do.

Don't Think About "Link Building", Think About Branding

We don't necessarily want to go after links with our keywords in them, we want people to link to your businesses website naturally, and that usually happens by your businesses name.

What do I mean by that?

Well, when you link to a website or they link to you, the words within that link are called anchor text. One of the major updates Google released recently is to slap sites with over optimized anchor text profiles.

Meaning these websites were actively going and getting other websites to link to them using keywords they wanted their website to rank for. In Google's eyes this is gaming their search engine.

This leads to overly optimized anchor texts and backlinks, which is a big no no.

It's really important to have a varied and diversified backlink anchor text profile and that's where branding comes into play.

When someone links to your website, it most likely won't be keyword based, it will be branding based, IE, the anchor text pointing to your site will most likely have your businesses name in it or something close to that.

This is considered natural to Google. So, first step is to forget all about 'buying backlinks'. You've probably seen offers for services where for X amount of money they will deliver you 100 backlinks.

No matter what they say, no matter how appealing that might sound to you, skip it. Move on, don't be tempted.

So what can you do outside of SEO to brand your business? Think about things like publicity or promotions or mentions of your business in newspapers.

I'm going to give you a couple of examples of ways I've helped clients get natural backlinks to their site from NON seo related activities.

Handyman In Brisbane – Local Directories / Forums

We did work for a company that hired out handymen to help people around the house. They got a percentage of every hour the handyman worked.

They were spending upwards of $400 a day on Google Adwords with CPC costs as high as $7 per click so they wanted us to work on their organic SEO rankings.

Given that their website was optimized well, our only goal was to get relevant backlinks to their site. In Australia, we have a lot of business directories. Most countries do, especially the USA and the UK.

Local business directories are great as they are a simple source of high quality backlinks.

We did a simple search for business directories in Australia as well as local directories in Brisbane and we added our clients site to as many of these directories as possible.

90% of them were free, 10% had a nominal one time fee.

We also found 5 forums that were related to DIY and home improvement in Australia simply by searching in Google.

The good thing about forums is, not only do you get a backlink back to your site in your signature line, you are also engaging with potential customers.

Our strategy here was simple. Get the business owner to answer questions people had that they knew the answer to and could give an informed view.

Not short, little unhelpful answers, but long, well explained answers to these peoples problems.

Where possible, we also got them to link to a section on their website explaining more about the process they were talking about.

The key here is not to be promotional. Don't even try and sell here, just inform. Most forums also allow for a signature line. A little byline at the end of each of your forum posts.

These are all valuable links back to your site.

With just business directories & forum backlinks, this client moved from page 3 for their major keyword to middle of page 1 and they were able to decrease their ad spend by 3/4.

This was for a very competitive keyword.

Hairdresser Miami – List's Of Top Businesses For Other Beauty Services

Shout outs are definitely not a new concept, but they work well for backlinks.

We took on work for a Hairdresser in Miami and one of the tactics we used was creating resource lists, linking to other local businesses and then letting those businesses know we had given them a shout out.

We created 4 lists and put them on our clients website.

For example, one list was about the top day spas in Miami and another list was on the best beauty salons in Miami. We wrote little descriptions of each business and why we liked them.

We then contacted those businesses, with a quick, 'hey, have a look at this email, we talked about you on our site', and we had a such a great response.

Businesses love to be recognized.

Soon enough, businesses were linking back to our clients website in reciprocation and also sharing our clients website on their Facebook and Twitter pages.

We ended up with over 20 quality local backlinks and thousands of Facebook likes.

This might not seem like a lot, but it's massive in the local space where 3 or 4 backlinks from related businesses websites in your area is often enough to rank for the toughest of keywords.

Most of these backlinks were branded backlinks, meaning they had the businesses name in the anchor text and linked back to their homepage.

Mobile App Creator - Haro

Publicity can be hard to find, so my theory has always been, put yourself in front of people who want to give you publicity to help themselves out.

This tends to be reporters and bloggers.

They always need content and they always need experts to interview and that's where Haro comes into play and this is what we did for a client who created mobile apps for businesses.

Our client created apps for businesses who wanted to have an app that their customers could use to access their products or services. It was a high end service in a very competitive market and they had a small advertising budget.

We needed to not only get them backlinks, but also traffic to their website, so we went with publicity.

Haro is short for Help A Reporter Out. They connect experts like yourself with media organizations, journalists and bloggers.

When a reporter needs a source for their next article, they come here to quote experts.

When they quote you, they often give you a link back to your website as well. These links are gold as they end up on some very big websites.

We set our client up as a source / expert of app creation and the mobile economy.

We created fir them a profile so reporters could see what expertise they had and we scanned the daily lists of topics reporters wanted to cover and sent them the relevant ones.

In a period of 60 days, they were sourced 4 times in articles or reports and ended up getting over 300 separate backlinks to their site.

If you have some expert knowledge, this is a great source of branding and link building.

Teeth Whitening Service In Adelaide – Free Teeth Whitening / Social Media

Social media shares, especially Facebook shares have become huge in terms of SEO rankings.

Websites and specific web pages on your site that have a good amount of Facebook likes, get better rankings than those who skip social media or who have a small presence.

One of our clients had a promotion on where they offered a free teeth whitening to you if you had a friend come in and pay for their teeth whitening. Essentially it was a half price offer.

The first thing we did was create a specific page about this deal on their website. We then added in the standard social media share bars you see on websites.

It allows visitors to like the page on Facebook and share the link on Twitter, without leaving the site. It also shows the amount of shares dynamically as well.

The next thing we did was send out the link to their small Facebook and Twitter followers. We asked them to share and like the page.

The offer went gangbusters.

They had a Facebook following of only around 250 people, but the page ended up with over 2000 Facebook likes and 75 Twitter shares.

Their website over the following few months shot up from literally no where, to the front page for most of their keywords, over all the site.

Not just the page with the shares, but their entire site got a massive boost from all these shares.

How To Build A Quick And Easy Social Media Presence For Better SEO Rankings Over Time

Social media is now playing quite a significant role in search engine rankings. This is only going to increase over time as social networks like Facebook and Twitter get even bigger.

In this section, I'm going to talk about what you can do with the traffic you have already to grow your social media profile.

Now that you have a perfectly optimized website and web pages for the keywords you want to target with great long content, it's time to get them buzzing on social media.

Let's say you have a page on Teeth Whitening In Miami. You obviously want to rank this page for your set of keywords you found earlier.

Social shares can push up your rankings quite significantly. I like to think of each page on your site as almost like a separate website.

It requires it's own content, it's own links and it's own social shares.

It's all well and good to have a lot of great links and social shares for your home page, but you want to get some of that targeted link juice pointing to your inner keyword pages.

The first thing you want to do is to get a social share bar on your website. You see these all the time on websites. It asks visitors to like and share the page on Facebook, Twitter, etc.

Every page you are wanting to rank for should have a social media share bar on it. Let me show you what I mean;

http://www.buzzfeed.com/jennaguillaume/this-post-may-contain-traces-of-sarcasm

BuzzFeed.com is a great example.

They have millions and millions of social shares. If you go to the link above, you will see that above the article, they have a share bar. The also have the bar floating down the page on the side and at the bottom of the article.

They know the power of social media.

You can add something like this to your site and you should. This will allow visitors to like your specific pages on Facebook & Twitter.

I'd recommend only using a small amount of social media sites. If you only use Facebook, that's fine as well.

The major social networks for most businesses will be Facebook & Twitter, and those with a focus on images, like wedding cakes or weddings or food or female products should add Pinterest as well as that is a very female focused social network.

How you go about putting one of these social bars on your site depends on how your site is built. If it's built with Wordpress, it's as simple as purchasing a plugin and installing it.

My favorite Wordpress plugin for this is;

http://codecanyon.net/item/easy-social-share-buttons-for-wordpress/6394476

There are however many free ones.

If your site is built with HTML or something similar to that, it will require someone to add in the code into your site. You will need to talk to your webmaster about this.

With my clients, I personally add a social bar at the top and bottom of the page.

Then over a few weeks period, I post a link to each page I want to rank for on their Facebook and Twitter pages to try and get as many likes and shares for each page.

Even a small amount of shares or likes can make a big difference to rankings. You want to get as many likes as possible. If that means hitting up friends and family to like your pages on Facebook, so be it.

If you have a small following already, even better. Over time you will collect more likes and shares from the visitors coming to your site organically.

Building Your Citations Easily

If your business has a retail or office presence, any physical presence really, you will want to start building citations as soon as possible.

As Moz.com puts it well;

"Citations are defined as mentions of your business name and address on other webpages—even if there is no link to your website. An example of a citation might be an online yellow pages directory where your business is listed, but not linked to.

Citations can also be found on local chamber of commerce pages, or on a local business association page that includes your business information, even if they are not linking at all to your website."

Citations are a big ranking factor in search engines like Google and Bing. They help them to find out that you are who you say you are, therefore relevant to their search results.

In non competitive niches, they can be all the "backlinking" you might need to do, but I like to call it branding more than backlinking.

It's all about building your brand. Everything I've taught so far in this book is about building your brand, not your website, not your traffic count, not your backlinks.

It's about branding you as the go to place for X in your area. That is how you dominate the search engines. Not through tricks, not through one off tactics.

Back to citations.

It can take hours to find all the places online that you should be getting citations from, or you can use a tool that does it for you.

Yes, it's a paid tool, but they have a free trial which is often more than enough for what you will need. If not, $20 right now buys you one month, and that one month is all you need.

The service is called WhiteSpark.

https://www.whitespark.ca/local-citation-finder

You type in a search term, like we have talked about earlier and your location and it finds you all the directories and places to get citations for your business that you could want.

All you have to do after that is add your site to these websites. It shows you also where your competitors are getting citations from. Just follow the steps you are given and you are done.

It will probably take you a few hours to do them all.

Add this with everything else you've learnt in this book and you have an unstoppable SEO force working for your business.

Most businesses, I'd say 99% of businesses don't know all of these tactics so you are miles ahead of the competition right now.

If you are looking for more citations that are more industry focused, Moz has another great list here;

https://moz.com/learn/local/citations-by-category

Google My Business &
The Importance Of Reviews

I've already touched on Google My Business earlier and how to set it up and why it's important for rankings. What I want to talk about now however is reviews.

This is mostly for local businesses, those who would show up in local searches that I talked about earlier.

When you see those My Business listings when you do a local search, you will also notice that some have reviews under them. This is what you want.

Not only does this make people want to click on your business more, it's also a big ranking factor in Google. You want to get as many reviews as possible from your customers.

5 minimum.

Why 5? Because when you hit 5 reviews, you get little stars under your businesses listing. This again attracts more attention to your business.

Reviews are social proof. Social proof is huge. When it comes to getting reviews, here are a few things to remember.

* Don't post fake reviews. Never do that.

* Do ask your followers on Facebook & Twitter to leave reviews

* Try and get 5 reviews as quickly as possible.

* To leave a review, someone must have a Google account, which is free

* Don't stop trying to get reviews after 5. Every few months, keep asking for honest reviews

SEO Resources & Articles Worth Reading

These resources and links below are not just filler content. I'd highly suggest reading the articles that I've linked to as they with add an extra element to your knowledge base.

Keyword Research:

SemRush.com

Google Keyword Planner

Duplicate Content Issues:

Make Sure You Don't Have Duplicate Content – Moz

Link Building:

Up To Date Link Building Strategies – Point Blank SEO

Definitive Guide To Link Building – Brian Dean

Local SEO:

Very Up To Date Local SEO Articles – Moz

The Basics:

Basics Of SEO – Moz

Useful Misc Tools & Resources:

Keep People From Stealing Your Content – Kiss Metrics

On Page SEO:

On Page Ranking Factors – Moz

Mobile SEO:

Increase Sales From Mobile Visits – Kiss Metrics

Conclusion

Hopefully, by now after finishing this book, you've worked out that doing your own SEO isn't that difficult. Small little tweaks can make a huge difference to your rankings.

You should also know by now that spending a fortune on SEO is just not needed.

If for some reason you are not comfortable doing the work in this guide yourself, find someone who has even the most basic knowledge of HTML, hire them for a day and get them to implement everything in this guide for you.

You will still end up saving thousands of dollars over hiring a company or expensive, on going service. I'd recommend looking at your local college or university or even placing a simple ad on somewhere like Gumtree.

The major point to take away from this is, to not bury your head in the sand and either say it's all too difficult to do at all or I'll just hire the work out to an expensive SEO service.

The value of SEO is immense. You can bring in thousands, tens of thousands, even hundreds of thousands of dollars of new revenue to your business with good rankings.

Free Download

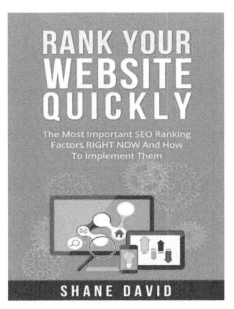

Hold On! Rank Your Website Even Quicker With This Free Gift

As a token of my gratitude for purchasing my ebook, I wanted to give you a small, but very valuable gift. I've been doing SEO full time now since 1998 and I know better than anyone else how quickly things change when it comes to SEO.

But there is one time proven strategy that always works and that ranks your website for the keywords that matter quickly.

Grab your free gift below and implement these strategies today. **You will learn;**

* The ONE strategy that will almost always guarantee you high rankings

* The new rules of SEO – Google knows more about your site than ever before

* An instant rank boosting SEO strategy that you can implement in minutes

http://thefulltimer.com/seo/

Made in the USA
Middletown, DE
29 May 2020

96318174R00056